LETTERS TO HENRIETTA

Other Cambridge Reading books you may enjoy

Heroes and Villains
Tony Bradman

Spindle River
Judith O'Neill

The Hermit Shell
Frances Usher

Letters to Henrietta

Nell Marshall

CAMBRIDGE
UNIVERSITY PRESS

Cambridge Reading

General Editors
Richard Brown and Kate Ruttle

Consultant Editor
Jean Glasberg

PUBLISHED BY THE PRESS SYNDICATE OF THE UNIVERSITY OF CAMBRIDGE
The Pitt Building, Trumpington Street, Cambridge CB2 1RP, United Kingdom

CAMBRIDGE UNIVERSITY PRESS
The Edinburgh Building, Cambridge CB2 2RU, United Kingdom   www.cup.cam.ac.uk
40 West 20th Street, New York, NY 10011-4211, USA   www.cup.org
10 Stamford Road, Oakleigh, Melbourne 3166, Australia
Ruiz de Alarcón 13, 28014 Madrid, Spain

Letters to Henrietta
Text © Nell Marshall 1998
Original artwork © Sam Thompson 1998
Maps © Jeff Edwards 1998
Picture Research by Sandie Huskinson-Rolfe of PHOTOSEEKERS.
Cover photograph and photographs of realia © Graham Portlock 1998

First published 1998
Reprinted 1999

Printed in the United Kingdom at the University Press, Cambridge

Typeset in Hollander and Trade Gothic

A catalogue record for this book is available from the British Library.

ISBN 0 521 47625 9 paperback

Acknowledgements
A Scottish Game of Croquet, (litho), by Alfred Concanen (19th century), Private Collection/Bridgeman Art Library, London/New York: p.14 *top*, Tanks, Somme (w/c), by Captain Edward Henry Handley-Read (1869–1935), Topham Picture Source/Bridgeman Art Library, London/New York: p.39; British Red Cross Museum and Archives: p.35; Cambridgeshire Collection/Cambridge Central Library: pp.16 *bottom*, 17 *bottom*; ET Archive: pp.23 *bottom*, 24 *bottom*; Mary Evans Picture Library: pp.21, 23 *middle*; Getty Images: pp.12, 15, 23 *top*, 26, 37 *top and bottom*, 38; 'The Trustees of the Imperial War Museum, London': pp.25, 41; Peter Newark's Historical Pictures: pp.23 *inset*, 24 *top*, 36; 'PA News': p.42; Pictor International: pp.42–43; Popperfoto: p.25 *inset*; Sygma L'Illustration p.39 *background*; Topham Picturepoint: pp.16 *inset*, 44 *bottom left*.

We have been unable to trace the copyright holder for the photograph on page 39 and would be grateful for any information that would enable us to do so.

Our special thanks to Repton School, Repton, Derbyshire, for granting us permission to use photographs on page 18.

All other photographs are courtesy of the author.

CONTENTS

HOW CAN WE KNOW ABOUT OUR FAMILIES IN THE PAST?

LETTERS

In 1978 Aunt Henrietta had a grand clear-out. She sent my husband a packet of letters she had kept for sixty years, which were written to her by her brother Henry. Henry was a soldier in the First World War, which took place between 1914 and 1918. These were special letters as they gave a first-hand account of what Henry had seen and done through four terrible years. Henrietta had kept letters from her other brothers too.

↘ One of the many letters Henrietta received from her brothers.

1842

Edward Marshall born

1857

Edward begins to keep his diary

1879

Edward Marshall marries Lucy Knight

1880–1889

Edward and Lucy's nine children born

1914

First World War begins

1915

Jack killed

191

Evel kille

↑ Edward Marshall's diary, showing the page for 1851

DIARIES

One day I found a book called 'Jefferson's Family Diary 1850–1950' among old family papers. A page for each year gave just enough space to write in important events. It had belonged to Edward, my husband's grandfather, who lived from 1842 to 1933. He had recorded family events like the date when he left school, his marriage, and the births of his children, as well as national events such as the outbreak of the First World War on 3 August 1914. We can corroborate many of these entries by checking them against other records such as birth certificates and newspaper reports. A diary like this is a very useful record of a family's past.

1918 End First World War

1923 Henry marries Dorothy Doyle

1925 Henry's son Geoffrey Marshall born

1957 Geoffrey Marshall marries Nell Sargant

1978 Henrietta sends the letters to Geoffrey and Nell

1998 Nell Marshall writes this book

PHOTOGRAPHS

Everyone enjoys looking at old photos and trying to work out who the people in them are. Most families have collections of photos of themselves and their homes. Some of these get lost, but many survive and are passed on to the next generation, showing us what the people and places really looked like.

⬎ Some of the photos of Henrietta and her family which have survived.

STORIES

Another way we can find out about the recent past is by listening to the stories people tell about their childhood, their parents and even their grandparents. Most families have favourite stories, and they are passed on, becoming a source of information about the past.

A JIGSAW

Finding out about the past is like doing a jigsaw. There are lots of different sorts of information or evidence – letters, diaries, photos and the stories people tell, as well as other records such as newspaper reports and government documents. We can put these things together to build up a picture of what people and their lives were like in the past.

HENRIETTA AND HER FAMILY

I have used all these things to make a picture of Henrietta and her family. They were an ordinary middle-class Victorian family growing up happily at the end of the nineteenth century. But the First World War brought terrible changes to their peaceful lives. This book tells you both about their childhood and about how, as adults, they faced those difficult times.

Some of the words in this book are old-fashioned or are words which are used only in the army. Definitions of these words appear in the glossary on pages 46–48.

Nell Marshall.

Jack in 1890

Edward 1842–1933

Jack in 1914

Evelyn in 1915

Henry and Henrietta in 1919

Nell Marshall

Henrietta in 1897

HENRIETTA'S FAMILY AND HOME

Henrietta Marshall was born in 1889. She was the youngest in a family of two girls and seven boys. The family tree shows that Edward Marshall (her father) married Lucy Knight (her mother) in 1879, and that each year between 1880 and 1889 (except in 1886) Lucy had a new baby. Nine children in ten years! How on earth did she manage?

Married

1 January 1879

Edward
Thory
MARSHALL

b. 26 July 1842

Lucy
Charlotte
Emma
KNIGHT

b. 17 August 1848

Frederic
Charles

2 February 1880

Charlie

Frances
Katherine
Lucy

2 August 1882

Arthur Patterson

25 September 1884

Artie

Evelyn
Saffrey

28 January 1887

Eve

Henrietta
Mary

21 July 1889

John
Edward

3 June 1881

Jack

Hannath
Arnold

20 August 1883

Hans

Russell
Hardy
Sidney

18 September 1885

Russ

Henry

26 February 1888

Hal

The babies were born at home. Lucy was attended by the midwife, and a person called the monthly nurse stayed in the house for a while to look after Lucy and the new baby. A nanny helped Lucy to bring up the children.

The Reverend Edward Marshall, Henrietta's father, was the vicar of St Andrew's Church in Sutton, a large village six miles (10 km) from Ely in East Anglia.

The vicarage where they all lived was a large rectangular house. It was approached by a gravel drive lined with lilac bushes and surrounded by two acres of gardens and orchards. This is about the size of two football pitches!

The house had no modern comforts like electricity, running hot and cold water and flushing toilets. Water for washing had to be heated and carried upstairs, and then the dirty water carried downstairs. Each bed had a chamber pot beneath it. Light was provided by oil lamps which had to be cleaned and filled each day. There was no heating in the bedrooms, and a coal fire was lit upstairs only in the nursery, or in a bedroom if someone was ill. In winter the children sometimes found the water frozen in their washbasins.

But there were servants to help with all the work: a cook and maid in the kitchen, a gardener and his boy for outside. Most important of all for Lucy and the children was the nanny, Elizabeth Field, who worked for them for many years. She was helped in the nursery by a series of young girls from the village. Most middle-class Victorian families had at least one servant, and many children were brought up by nannies.

Outside, the children had plenty of space to play. In the picture you can see that the lawn is set up for croquet. The gardener was kept busy looking after the lawn and working in the greenhouse, where grapes and peaches were grown. In the kitchen gardens grew all the vegetables and fruit the family needed.

The family kept chickens, a cow for milk and a pig. When the time came for the pig to be killed, the children were sent out for the day and the butcher was called to kill the pig and chop it up. The bacon and ham were kept hanging in the spacious larder.

GROWING UP

There were nine children in Henrietta's family. This would be a large number for any mother to look after on her own, but fortunately for Lucy the children were brought up partly by their nurse. It was usual for middle-class Victorian children to be brought up by a nurse or nanny, and for them to see their parents only at certain times of the day. The children had their own room in the house, the nursery, which was where they passed most of their time until they were old enough to go to school. They would see their mother and father at meals and at prayers in the morning, but otherwise they might not see their parents for the rest of the day.

↓ This is a Victorian family, rather like Henrietta's, at family prayers.

At 9.30 each morning family prayers were held in the dining room for all the family and servants. This was often the only time the children saw their father, partly because he was so busy with his work. To the children he was almost a stranger, writing sermons in his study, or out in the village visiting his parishioners. The children never approached their father directly, but used their mother as a go-between. The children were never as close to their father as they were to each other and their mother.

In many ways, the children's lives were like the lives of children today – they played together, went to school and so on – but the details were rather different! This picture, taken in 1890, shows Arthur, aged five, sitting on a cross between a bicycle and a rocking horse. He would have been proud of his sailor suit, as, until the boys were five, they were dressed in girl's clothes and their hair was left uncut. Their fifth birthday marked a step in the journey out of the nursery. When the boys were seven or eight they were sent away to their preparatory school, and at thirteen they went to public school. Charlie (10) and Jack (9) (standing with the bicycle) were probably home for their holidays.

Since earliest times, babies and young children wore skirts (possibly for warmth) until boys were 'breeched' (put into trousers or breeches) between five and seven years old. The development of boys' clothes for under-fives was encouraged by women's magazines in the twentieth century.

ACTIVITIES AND ADVENTURES

There were so many children in the family that there was always someone to play with, but Henrietta, Frances and their brothers did have to make their own entertainment. There were no televisions, cinemas or radios, and books were far more expensive than they are today. But there were plenty of other things to do. Football was a favourite with the boys, and in the summer they all played tennis and croquet on the lawn.

> Croquet was invented in France over 700 years ago. It involves using mallets to knock balls through a series of hoops laid out on a lawn. You can also knock your opponents' balls away. Croquet is still played today, but it was particularly popular in the nineteenth century.

By the age of ten each child could ride a bicycle, and they often rode six miles into Ely, or even the fifteen miles into Cambridge, making the most of the flat fen landscape around Sutton. It was exciting returning in the dark. Bicycle lamps were lit with acetylene gas, which sometimes exploded!

> A fen is a low, marshy piece of land. The fens in East Anglia, where the Marshall family lived, have been drained by a network of canals or drains since the seventeenth century.

The children were encouraged to sketch and paint. This is a picture by Frances of Sutton church. A small gate from the vicarage garden led into the churchyard. In the picture, Henrietta is playing tennis, while her mother snatches a well-earned snooze.

This picture shows a game of croquet in progress.

a family story

Evelyn and Henry did everything together. When they were nine and eight they woke one morning to see that everything had frozen hard. After breakfast, with their skates, but without telling anyone, they set off. They started skating on one of the many drains around Sutton, and just kept going. The dog, who had followed them, soon gave up running along the bank, and went home. By early afternoon, they realised they were miles from home. They turned round to skate back, and darkness fell. Meanwhile, at the vicarage, the boys' absence was noticed at lunch time and, when the exhausted dog returned alone, Lucy and Edward were alarmed. A search party from the village set off. Both parents were convinced the boys had drowned because the drains were dangerous for skating. Wherever they were crossed by a bridge, the ice beneath was sheltered, and not so hard. As the boys made their way back, they saw the lights of the search party bobbing towards them.

Their father successfully hid any relief he felt at finding the boys and said, "You have behaved badly and, indeed, you have broken your mother's heart." When they reached home, Lucy greeted them with sobs of relief, and when they were out of earshot of Edward she said, "You realise, of course, that you have broken your father's heart."

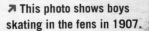
↗ This photo shows boys skating in the fens in 1907.

SCHOOL – AT HOME AND AWAY

The children were taught to read and write in the nursery by their mother, and then the boys went to a small local school. At the age of seven or eight, they were sent away to a preparatory boarding school. Evelyn and Henry were lucky as they were allowed to start their school at the same time – when Henry was eight and Evelyn was nine.

a family story

The school chosen for the boys was the Llandaff Choir School in south Wales. They did the long journey there on their own by train. Leaving Sutton at six in the morning by horse-drawn trap, they caught the train from Ely to Cambridge. They were entrusted to the care of the railway guard, who in those days travelled on every train. At Cambridge, he saw them onto the London train, and they were met at King's Cross by an aunt, who took them across London to Paddington. Once again, they were put into the care of the guard on the Cardiff train, and he put them onto the train from Cardiff to the small town of Llandaff. They arrived at nine o'clock in the evening, to be met by the headmaster. He looked cross and annoyed and said, "You're late! If this wasn't the first time you've done this journey, I'd beat you both."

Both boys were good at football and before long they were in the school team. In the photograph Henry is sitting at the left-hand end of the row, with Evelyn standing behind him.

While the boys were sent away to school so young, Frances and Henrietta did not go away until they were in their teens. They had lessons at home, but were also expected to help Lucy visiting sick people in the village, taking them beef tea and broth.

They also went with Lucy to the village school, which was attended by over two hundred children. The school log book records frequent visits when Lucy, Frances and Henrietta would look at the children's work, or listen to them sing or recite. On special occasions like Ascension Day the children would be rewarded with a 'scramble'. The school children would walk to the vicarage lawn and stand in a large circle. The teachers, Lucy, Henrietta and Frances would throw handfuls of sweets into the circle, and the children would literally 'scramble' for them. On May Day a maypole would be put up on the vicarage lawn for the schoolchildren to dance round.

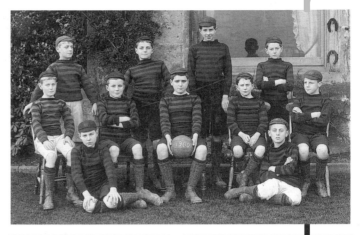

Why didn't the Marshall children go to the village school?

At that time, state education was only provided up to the age of fourteen, and children whose parents could afford to pay for their education weren't expected to go to state schools.

The school in Sutton was run by the Church of England. The vicar's family visited it to see how the pupils were getting on with their schoolwork and to encourage both the children and the teachers. Henrietta and Frances would not have been expected to be friendly with the children at this school: they were from a different social class, and richer and poorer children did not mix.

⬇ **The artist has imagined how a scramble might look.**

⬆ **Sutton school and all its pupils about a hundred years ago.**

At thirteen the boys went to a public school, called Repton, in Derbyshire, where their father and grandfather had gone. They played a lot of games, especially football, and studied Latin, English, History and Maths, but no Science. The school was divided into seven or eight 'houses'. Each one was looked after by a house master and a matron; at Repton the matrons were always known as 'dames'. Within each house, the boys were in 'studies'. Two or three boys would share a study.

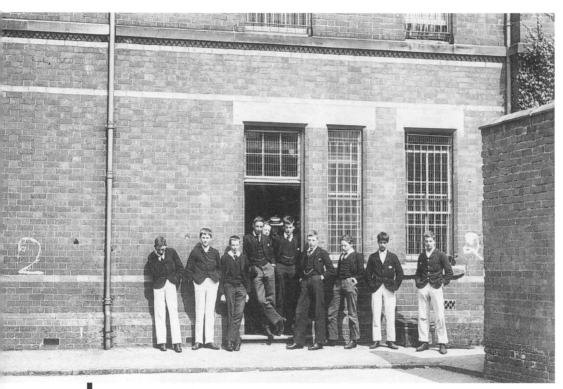

The top picture is of Repton at about the time the Marshall boys went there and below is one of Repton today.

It was at this time that Henrietta began to write to her brothers while they were away at school, and they sometimes wrote back to her. Here is a letter to Henrietta from Evelyn – it is the earliest letter to Henrietta that has survived.

Repton, Oct 7th

Dear Baby,

Thank you so much for your letter. Henry begins fagging tomorrow, and I leave off thank goodness! I expect Frances will have most of the stamps I sent her, you may have all she has not got. Have you heard yet whether Hans has got through any of his exams yet. I suppose Art finished off the tree before going back to Malvern. Have your lessons begun yet? In the Yard Fours (Footer) Henry and Russell are in the best [team?] and ought to get a Pot (Cup) each, our study will look quite smart (not Russ and H but the Pots). Don't you think I am getting rather funny. Prayer bell has just gone.

In bed at 9.20. On Michaelmas Day we had six geese, everybody had two go's, for my second help I was given a whole leg. I did my best but could not manage it all. Give my love to Jack and and all the others at home.

Ever your loving brother Stinkpot.

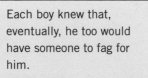
↑ **Evelyn's letter to Henrietta.**

A common custom at all public schools was that of fagging. Each younger boy was attached to an older boy in his house and had to fag for him, which meant running messages, cleaning shoes, making toast and tea or any other little job the older boy wanted doing.

Each boy knew that, eventually, he too would have someone to fag for him.

Meanwhile Henrietta did lessons at home and helped Lucy with duties in the village. At fifteen she went away to school in Winchester for a year and then returned to live at home. A job or career for her was not even thought about. She was expected to help her mother at home until she married, as Frances did in 1912. But as each of her seven brothers reached eighteen, they left school and started on their careers.

LEAVING HOME

By the time they were eighteen, the boys, who had already lived away from home for most of each year, were independent and ready to leave home altogether.

This photograph of the family was taken on 20 August 1897, which was Hannath's fourteenth birthday. It was the very last time they were all together. In September Charlie, at the back with his arms resting on the seat, not quite eighteen years old, sailed to Ceylon (now Sri Lanka) to join the colonial civil service as a police officer. He did not return to England until 1907, and by that time his brothers had all left home. Next to him is Jack, who was sixteen and in his last year at Repton. In the centre next to Lucy sits Arthur, nearly thirteen, and next to him Frances, just fifteen. To the right of Lucy is Russell, nearly twelve, and standing at the end is Evelyn, ten.

On the rug are Henry, nine, and Henrietta, eight, leaning against Hannath, who is holding onto the dog Billie.

They do not look very cheerful. It is as if they had all been told to put on their best clothes and behave themselves. If you look at Edward's nose, you will see it is covered in plaster. His diary records an accident on his tricycle as he rode around the village on 14 August, and this was the result.

After Charlie had gone, the other boys, one by one, left home too. By the time Frances got married in 1912, the boys were scattered to all parts of the British Empire. Jack joined the army and served in South Africa, Hong Kong, Malta and Sierra Leone. Evelyn worked as a mining engineer in the South African gold-fields. Russell, a doctor, went to the Solomon Islands as a medical missionary. Hannath worked in South Africa as an Anglican priest. Artie was a rubber planter in Malaya, and Charlie had been in Ceylon, Johore (Malaya) and the Straits Settlements (Malaya) as a civil servant.

Henry was the only one who did not go very far. Not only did his parents seem to have run out of names by the time he was born (he had only one, while the others had two or three!), but by the time he was grown up, they had run out of money too. Henry longed to be a doctor, but there was no money left to send him to university, so in 1906 he went to work in the Bank of England, a job which he loathed.

Henrietta was the only one left at home. She enjoyed writing to each brother once or twice a month, and carefully kept the letters they sent back.

At this time Britain ruled many countries that had once been independent and which are independent again today. It was common for young men to work in Britain's colonies, as civil servants, in the army, or taking advantage of the business opportunities that the Empire provided.

Very few women from middle-class families had careers at this time. They were expected to remain at home to help their families until they married. However, many British women, whether married or not, had some kind of paid work – as servants, or in factories, for example. Most people started work at the age of fourteen.

Canada

Britain
•Sutton

•Malta (*Jack*)

AFRICA

India

•Hong Kong (*Jack*)

Solomon Islands (*Russell*)

Sierra Leone (*Jack*)

Ceylon (*Charlie*)

Malaya (*Artie and Charlie*)

Australia

South Africa (*Jack, Evelyn and Hannath*)

The British Empire

Most of Henrietta's brothers spent the years before the First World War in different parts of the British Empire.

↑ This woman is running a spinning machine. She would have worked for twelve hours a day, six days a week.

THE FIRST WORLD WAR

When war broke out in August 1914 between Britain, France and Russia on one side and Germany, Austria-Hungary and Turkey on the other, people had no idea of how terrible it would be. By 11 November 1918, nine million soldiers had died, about 5,600 deaths for each day of the war. Millions of civilians suffered too – from hunger, disease, death of loved ones and homelessness.

⬇ The reasons for the war are very complicated, but it involved so many people because so many countries had made promises to defend each other.

How the two sides lined up during the First World War.

Germany and Austria-Hungary Allies

Britain, France and Russia Allies

Neutral countries

In Britain the declaration of war was greeted enthusiastically. In the early years of the century, Britain and Germany were fierce rivals, and many Britons were glad of the chance to fight Germany. Young men like Henry and Evelyn rushed to enlist in the army, wanting to be involved and afraid that the war would be over by Christmas. People thought that Germany, who had built up a large navy, overrun 'gallant little Belgium' and invaded France, should be taught a lesson.

Although the British army had been involved in various conflicts around the world, the country had not fought a major war for over fifty years. Then, soldiers on horseback (the cavalry) had charged into battle with drawn swords. The guns used were clumsy

↑ This crowd of people in the streets of London was photographed at the declaration of war in 1914.

The way wars were fought changed dramatically over a short period of time: the painting on the left shows a battle in 1854 during the Crimean War, and the painting below shows an attack on a German trench in 1918.

and slow to reload. The First World War saw the use of mustard gas for the first time, and the introduction of new weapons like the tank. Modern, improved guns could fire rapidly. This war was the first to be fought on land, at sea and in the air, with aeroplanes used for both reconnaissance and bombing. At sea, German submarines attacked convoys of ships bringing much-needed food and fuel to Britain.

The way in which battles were fought changed, and soldiers found themselves dug into trenches facing the enemy in *their* trenches across no man's land. Few people in August 1914 had expected that the war would be like this.

The main areas of battle were in France and Belgium, along the Russian borders, in Gallipoli (part of Turkey) and in the Middle East. In 1917, the Russians surrendered, following a revolution in their country, but the Americans joined the British and French. The Americans' input of soldiers and supplies, together with blockades which prevented food supplies getting into Germany, proved too much for Germany, who surrendered on 11 November 1918.

The British regular army was composed of volunteer soldiers led by highly trained officers, like Jack, who had made the army their career. The other armies – German, Russian, French, Austro-Hungarian and Turkish – were made up of conscript soldiers led by career officers. Young men in those countries were forced to spend time in the army. Britain did not introduce conscription until 1916, and relied at the start of the war on young men like Evelyn and Henry volunteering to fight. Britain started the war with a force of 150,000 men, known as the British Expeditionary Force. Most of the men were Privates and Corporals, known as 'other ranks'. However, Henrietta's brothers were all officers.

Henrietta's other brothers – Charlie, Arthur, Russell and Hannath – also wanted to take part in the war. Hannath did join a regiment as a chaplain, and Russell was an army doctor, but Charlie and Arthur were told that their jobs were too important to the war effort to give up. Only Jack, Evelyn and Henry took part in the fighting.

⬆ This photograph shows some of the first soldiers to go to France in 1914.

'No man's land' was what the soldiers called the area between the German trenches and the French and British trenches, because it was not controlled by either side. Areas of no man's land stretched from the Swiss border to the English Channel.

⬇ This painting shows the Somme battlefield in northern France. This is part of the landscape created by the war. You can see the trenches and the barbed wire in no man's land.

JACK'S WAR
JANUARY–MARCH

Jack was one of the few soldiers in 1914 who had any experience of fighting. He had been a soldier since 1901 and was a Lieutenant in the Duke of Cornwall's Light Infantry Regiment.

At first the Germans had done well, marching through Belgium into France, but there had been a great battle at the River Marne in September 1914, and the German army was halted by the French and British. Both sides dug themselves into trenches and the war came to a standstill while the two sides shot at each other across no man's land.

Officers had dugouts in the trenches – shelters dug into the side of the trench – but the ordinary soldiers simply lived in the trench for days at a time. The trenches were often overrun by rats, and there was no shelter from rain, snow or heat.

Jack's regiment was sent to trenches in Belgium.
Henrietta received many letters from him:

Jan 3rd 1915

Four days ago I was wired for to go back to my old battalion who have had most of their captains killed. I am actually 2nd in Command, so you can realise how many officers we have lost. We do 48 hours in the firing line & then a day in support. Of course food can only be got up at night, & wounded taken away & so on. Shelling is incessant all day, & I am quite used to it now, at first it's rather beastly. One shell burst on the parapet & buried 4 men & we got them all out alive. The trench I command is only 500 yards from the enemy's trenches, so things are pretty lively. I have not washed or shaved since I left the other battalion, or had my boots or clothes off.

France 6.1.15

We have just been relieved by another regiment in the firing line & are now in billets in a town for 5 days of rest, after which we return to the trenches again. The sheer damned discomfort of this trench is the limit. You are under shell fire all day, & the moment it gets dark you set to work and repair damages, digging till dawn, when you get shelled again.

Jack wrote to Henrietta every week. The post to the front lines from England was efficient, and there are many references to the food parcels he was so grateful to receive. He also asked for things he wanted sent.

> **6.1.15**
>
> You might send me some thin socks to put under my thick ones, my feet swell so I can't put two pairs of thick ones on.

> **26.1.15**
>
> Please send me my left-handed scissors, as I have not been able to cut my nails yet, and my fingers are so dirty in trenches I can't bite them, so get a move on.

> **13.2.15**
>
> The cakes were tophole & a most convenient size to take into a trench. Please don't send any more shortbread, socks, or chocolate, as we have tons now in the mess, where food is more or less pooled. Small things like sardines, oxo, & potted meat are always useful, big parcels are the devil to get into a trench.

Jack knew that German snipers would be looking out for British officers, and that he was more likely to be a target than the other soldiers. He must also have known that Henrietta loved him enough that she would not think badly of him for being frightened.

This was a big admission to make: people at home often liked to think of their sons and brothers as heroes who could never be scared.

> **20.2.1915**
>
> I lost my woolly cap last night on an officer's patrol near the German lines, & I was too frightened to go back for it. If any of your knitting parties have one to spare, I should rather like it. One always wears a cap on patrol, the ordinary officer's cap gives one away at once, and no one hates being shot at more than I do.

On 29 March 1915, Jack wrote his last letter:

> I relieve Capt Hughson's Company in the advanced trench tonight, much to my disgust as there are very strong suspicions of a mine in it & no one likes being hoisted into the air on these cold nights & then rushed almost before you have come down. No time for more, best love to you all, Ever your loving Jack.

Jack's suspicions about the mine were correct, for he was killed in action the next day, 30 March 1915, not yet thirty-four years old.

➔ Jack's death was the first death due to the war that Edward Marshall recorded in his diary.

Memorable ⚜ 1915 ⚜ Events.

MO.	DAY	EVENT
Jan.	1	H.M.S. Formidable sunk
	19	German airship over Norfolk
	24	Dogger Bank Battle
	25	E.S.M., 2nd Lt. Royal Warwickshire Regt.
Feb.	2	Turks defeated on Suez Canal.
	5	Army estimates for 3000 000 men.
	18	Blockade of England commanded.
	25	Entrance to Dardanelles shelled.
Mar.	14	Mrs Pheard died.
	10	Capture of Neuve Chapelle.
	22	Russians take 120 000 prisoners & 700 guns at Przemsl.
	30	J.E.M. killed in Action.
Apr.	7	Henry's Battery, H.A.C., left Mundesley for the Front.
	16	Bombs on E. Kent, Essex & Suffolk.
	22	Asphyxiating gases used by Germans.
May	3	George Harris Sea died.
	4	3rd War Budget. £1,132,654,000.
	23	Italy was our Ally
		Cunard Lusitania sunk near Queenstown
Jun.	19	E.S.M. Lieut. R.War. R., sailed with Medit. Exp. Force
	3	Premysl re-taken from Russia
	4	British & French land on Gallipoli.
	22	Lemberg re-taken fm. Russia.
	29	Fred. Jash Dickinson died.
July	15	Lt. J.C.A. Burt, R.F.A., killed in Battle of the Somme, at. 25. vide Oct: 26. 1917.
Aug.	21	Italy declares War on Turkey.
	6	new landing at Suvla Bay.
	18	Russian victory in Riga gulf.
Sep.	7	E.S.M. Capt. R.War. R.
	13	L.C.E.M. operation for appendicitis by Dr Cook.
	20	Her nurse left
	25-27	Gal: British & French successes: Germans driven back on 2nd line.
Oct.	14	Bulgaria at war with Serbia.
	5	Allied Forces land at Salonica.
Nov.	5	Fall of Nish.
	29	British with-drawal from Ctesiphon.
Dec.	12	Confirmation in Sutton Ch. 19 M. 20 F.
	28	E.S.M.'s Brigade evacuated Helles.
Nov.	27	Louisa Vehan died.
Dec.	15	Sir Douglas Haig succeeds Sir John French.
	19	Anzac & Suvla Bay evacuated

← These are the medals awarded to Jack for his participation in the war.

EVELYN'S WAR

Evelyn was commissioned as a Second Lieutenant in the Royal Warwickshire Regiment in January 1915. His regiment left for the Dardenelles in June to fight Turkey, an ally of Germany. The aim of the campaign was to help Britain's ally, Russia, who was blockaded by Turkey at the Dardenelles. Casualties on the British side amounted to over a quarter of a million men.

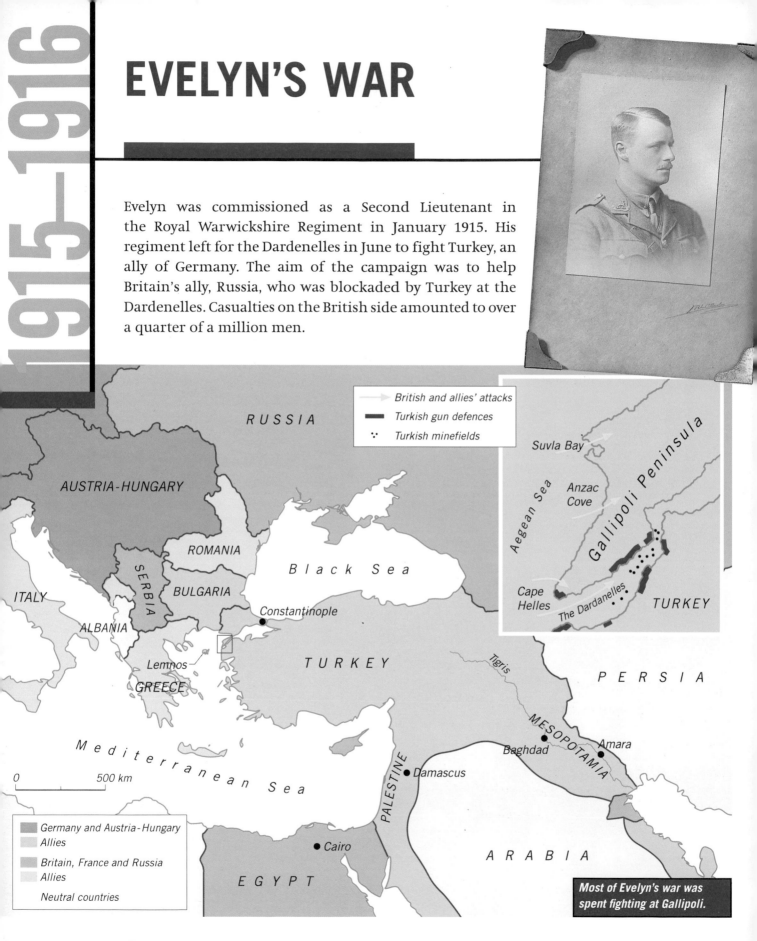

British and allies' attacks
Turkish gun defences
Turkish minefields

RUSSIA

Suvla Bay

Aegean Sea

Anzac Cove

Gallipoli Peninsula

AUSTRIA-HUNGARY

ROMANIA

Black Sea

SERBIA

BULGARIA

Constantinople

Cape Helles

The Dardanelles

TURKEY

ITALY

ALBANIA

Lemnos

GREECE

TURKEY

Tigris

PERSIA

M e d i t e r r a n e a n   S e a

MESOPOTAMIA

Baghdad

Amara

PALESTINE

Damascus

0   500 km

Cairo

ARABIA

Germany and Austria-Hungary Allies
Britain, France and Russia Allies
Neutral countries

EGYPT

Most of Evelyn's war was spent fighting at Gallipoli.

Evelyn's letters give a vivid picture of this dreadful campaign:

> *Monday July 19th 1915*
>
> We were lying by the sea for 2 days then went up to the firing line & have had 48 hours there. It's most awfully hard & trying work & the smell! Several times a day I have dug up bodies that have only been partially buried. This is worse than France a lot – no water, food bad. I haven't washed or had my boots off since leaving the Beach. Shrapnel is awful, one shell buried me under a parapet, but didn't do any harm – shells & rifle fire are passing over all the time.

> *14/8/15*
>
> On Thursday I came back to duty from Lemnos. First thing I was told was that I was the only officer left in the Battn. The Battn has 280 left out of 1018. I am at present commanding "D" Coy which numbers exactly 38 – out of 220. All the officers killed or wounded. If you hear anyone saying he is dying to come out – tell him not to worry – he will die quick enough out here. I haven't washed, shaved, cleaned my teeth or changed clothing since I have been up here. We work day & night and sudden death is always blowing about. Bully beef, biscuits, & milk & sugarless tea or plain water is our food for every meal.
>
> P.S. Your air cushion is my constant companion and worth its weight in gold.

In the midst of all the horror, Evelyn managed to write cheerfully, and the smallest pleasures became very important:

> *3rd Sept 1915*
>
> We are well out of the firing line & close to the sea & my Coy gets a bathe every day – going down in small numbers so as not to attract shell fire. Great treat yesterday, we got a little bit of fresh meat & vegetables. We walk over a few sand dunes down to the sea & there are some really lovely white lilies growing there – four heads on a stalk – white & long with a scent like a Tuber rose. We picked a large bunch this morning & have them in an old jam tin.

The campaign went from bad to worse. It was decided to withdraw troops from Gallipoli at Suvla Bay, and by Christmas all supplies and many of the troops had been moved out. Evelyn's letter of 20 January 1916 shows that he played an important role:

Evelyn spent the next month in Egypt. He wanted above everything else to get some home leave, but it was not to be, and he wrote bitterly on 7 February:

> *I need hardly say how sick I am about losing my leave – I had set my heart on it – I can't write about it.*

> *Dear Old Girl,*
>
> *I know I haven't written for the 'ell of a time – they wouldn't let me in case any of the details of the Suvla evacuation should reach the enemy. We did it all right & I had the honour & glory of commanding the last party of 50 men who held the line for a day & a half after the main body had gone & finally the last night held it with 25 men after the Rear Party had gone.*
>
> *We are now on the "Simla" in harbour at Mudros waiting to go to Egypt – whether for a rest or more endless fighting we don't know – we are all tired and don't care what happens.*

His regiment was sent to Mesopotamia, and on 27 February 1916 Evelyn wrote that they expected to land the next day and continue up the River Tigris in small boats:

We are just getting in sight of the Persian Hills away on our right. The country is nice and green & pleasant here, but above Amara where we are going, it's all desert and not a blade of cover anywhere. The Turks are all heavily entrenched – I hope the Russians will get a move on & harass them in the back.

The letter of 27 February was his last to Henrietta. On 20 March he wrote to his mother:

We are in for something big, and accidents do happen even in the best regulated battles & if anything should happen to me – please don't put on mourning – but rather hold up your head the higher – for after all there is nothing to grieve over. I shall be quite happy. We shall hammer the Turks all right – we are all confident of that & there will be casualties, but that doesn't matter if our side wins.

➜ Evelyn's death was reported in the *Anglian Times*.

On the night of 4 April Evelyn was worried about some of his men, wounded and lying out in no man's land. He knew if they were found by the Turks they would be killed. He prepared to go and search for them. His batman begged him not to, but when Evelyn insisted, the batman said he would go with him. Evelyn ordered him not to, but the batman disobeyed, and he and Evelyn went out together in the dark. While searching for the wounded men, they disturbed a Turkish patrol, and Evelyn was shot in the stomach. His batman carried him back, but he died of his wound two days later, his men all wanting to stay by his stretcher during that time.

THE LATE CAPT. E. S. MARSHALL.
Officers' Tributes.

In General Monro's recently published despatch from the Dardanelles, we saw with pleasure that the late Captain Evelyn S Marshall, 9th Royal Warwickshire Regiment, son of Canon Marshall, Sutton in-the-Isle, was specially mentioned for gallant and distinguished conduct in the field.

In acquainting Canon Marshall of his son's death, Colonel Gordon expressed the deep sorrow of his fellow officers, and said: "We are all most deeply grieved. He led his company most gallantly at Falahiych (El Hannel), and in no small measure contributed to the brilliant success and capture of the Turkish trenches.

He was one of the noblest men I have ever known, brave (to a fault), modest, warm-hearted, cheerful when everyone else was depressed, enduring, and the most capable leader of men. His company was devoted to him, and all wanted to stay by him on his stretcher."

A brother officer wrote: "At Suvla, when most people fell sick, he was one of the mainstays of the Battalion, and kept things going when most others were ready to give in. I can remember how at one time he hung on with great grit against an overcoming sickness which would have sent others down to the hospital ship."

Another letter says: "All his men worshipped him, and would have followed him anywhere."

An officer wounded on Gallipoli tells how Capt. Marshall practically saved his life by ripping the fleecy lining out of his own coat, and sending him down to the hospital in it.

THE HOME FRONT

The telegram boy cycling up the vicarage drive was a sight Henrietta and her parents dreaded. There were few telephones, and the news that someone had been killed or wounded would be sent to the next of kin by telegram. It would be followed by letters of condolence from the man's senior officer. The family would wear mourning for some months, or at the very least a black armband. The deaths of Jack and Evelyn, just a year apart, were a tremendous blow to the family. They would not have had the comfort of a funeral and a grave to visit. Families were encouraged to take pride in the 'sacrifice' their men had made in 'laying down their lives for their country'. A letter Henrietta received from an uncle after Evelyn's death shows this:

What can I say? You know how I feel for you all — I believe I thought more of Evelyn than of any one else of his age — he was simply splendid & I think you should be proud to have had two such brothers as Jack & Evelyn to give their all for the cause we are all fighting for.

There was no television or radio, so people followed the events of the war through the newspapers. The entries in Edward Marshall's diary show that he recorded all the important events alongside entries about domestic happenings.

↑ Edward's diary for 1916. Evelyn's death is entered alongside events like Russell's marriage, wind damage to a church window, and important developments in the war.

People would also know about the war from the letters written by their sons, husbands and brothers, although letters written by soldiers had to be censored in case any information that might help the enemy fell into the wrong hands.

↖ **This post card has been censored.**

A. F. A. 2042
114/Gen. No./5248

FIELD SERVICE POST CARD

Miss Henrietta Marshall
Sutton Vicarage
Ely Cambs
England

NOTHING is to be written on this side except the date and signature of the sender. Sentences not required may be erased. If anything else is added the post card will be destroyed.

I am quite well.

I have been admitted into hospital { sick } and am going on well. { wounded } and hope to be discharged soon.

I am being sent down to the base.

I have received your { letter dated_____ { telegram_____ { parcel ,, _____

Letter follows at first opportunity.

I have received no letter from you { lately. { for a long time.

Signature only. } G. J. Marshall

Date 9/12/15

[Postage must be prepaid on any letter or post card addressed to the sender of this card.]

(b10558) Wt. W 3497-293. 860m. 5/15. S. & S.

Henrietta, who was twenty-five in 1914, remained at home throughout the war. Edward continued with his duties as the vicar in Sutton, although he was over seventy. As well as supporting her elderly parents, writing to her seven brothers each week, shopping for the things they asked for, and packing up and posting the parcels, Henrietta worked as a voluntary nurse at the Military Hospital in Ely, cycling there and back every day.

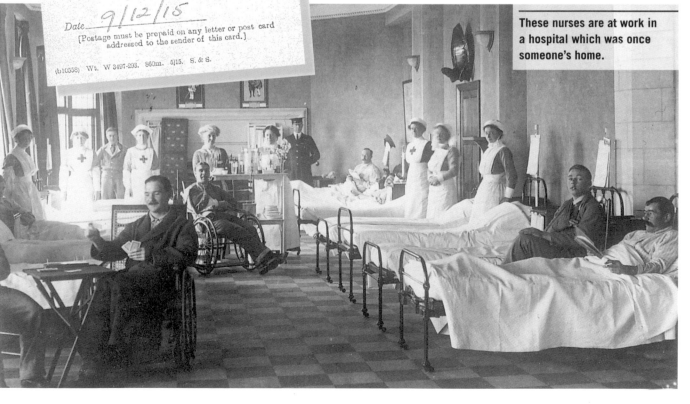

These nurses are at work in a hospital which was once someone's home.

Here is one of the hundreds of letters Henrietta wrote. It was sent to Evelyn, but for some reason it was never delivered and was sent back to her:

Feb 1916

We've had quite an excitement over Zepps this week. Six or seven came blowing over on Monday and one had the nerve to come here – lost its way I s'pose. We heard the old beast about 10 o'clock, and all rushed out and gaped at it. It made a noise like a young express, but it was darkish and we could see nothing, whereat we gaped the more. However it dropped no "bombs" on us – tho' over 300 were dropped in different places – 59 killed and 101 injured, which the papers describe cheerfully as "no considerable damage done" – I wonder what those 101 say!

As the war continued, more soldiers were needed, and in 1916 conscription was introduced. Young men were called up and had no choice but to join the army. With so many men away fighting, women took their place in factories and offices, often enjoying the freedom this gave them from domestic life. For many women, this was the first time such jobs had been open to them.

These women, working in factories in 1917, are doing jobs which would not have been open to them before the war.

← Zeppelins were airships which were used to bomb parts of England. Bombing was not nearly so extensive in the First World War as it was in the Second, since Zeppelins had a limited flying range. This was the first war in which civilians had been bombed from the air.

By 1916, it was clear that the war would not end quickly, and everyone knew someone who had been killed or wounded. The enthusiasm that had greeted the war in 1914 had gone.

HENRY'S WAR

Unlike Jack and Evelyn, who had belonged to infantry regiments, Henry had joined the Honourable Artillery Company (HAC). In the First World War, field guns were horse-drawn, and horses played an important part in an artillery regiment. Henry loved horses, and had ridden whenever he could before the war.

← An artillery gun being moved during the Battle of the Somme in 1916.

Routes from Britain to India and Australia after 1870

Suez Canal (*completed 1869*)

Egypt

India

AFRICA

To Australia

Cape of Good Hope

0   2000 km

← The Suez Canal was the most direct route for supplies of important goods like tea, cotton and rubber to get to Britain. If British ships had been unable to use it, they would have had to take the much longer and more dangerous route round the southern tip of Africa.

In April 1915, Henry was a Private in the HAC looking after horses in Egypt. The British army was in Egypt to defend the Suez Canal, the vital link for Britain with most of her Empire. Henry spent a year in Egypt, which he found dull as there was little action, and a great deal of desert, camels, flies, heat and dust.

In April 1916, Henry was summoned by his commanding officer and was handed an open telegram with the words, "I don't think this is very important." It contained the news of Evelyn's death and was a tremendous blow to Henry. He and Evelyn had been as close as twins since childhood, having started school together and shared many adventures such as their trip on the ice. Henry immediately applied for a commission, and for a transfer to fight in France. In July he was transferred to the Royal Field Artillery as a Second Lieutenant. He arrived in France in the middle of the Battle of the Somme, the most terrible battle of the war, which lasted five months and in which 1,256,000 British, French and German soldiers were killed. It was during this battle that tanks were used for the first time.

← Part of the Somme battlefield. The number of soldiers killed in this battle is about a quarter of the current population of Scotland.

Henry wrote regularly to Henrietta, addressing her as 'Dear Old Thing'.

He kept his letters light-hearted. Sixty years later, Henry still had nightmares about the battles he had fought in, but you would not think from his letters that he was writing from the thick of the most terrible battles in history.

Henry was also capable of joking about the horrible living conditions he and the other soldiers put up with. Here is a picture he drew of his dugout. This was a hole in the ground in which he lived while he was in the trenches. The comments around the edge of the picture show that Henry hadn't lost his sense of humour.

19 Nov 1916.

Thanks muchly for the socks, gloves & bullseyes. They were all excellent. Leave has opened, but that does not mean you will see me yet awhile, so don't count on it. although I have been out for 3 months & 2 days now. Some people have had no leave for 9 months, & I am naturally last on the list. Here is my menu. Breakfast porridge, bacon (sometimes an egg too) bread & marmalade (& generally ration butter). Lunch hot meat of sorts & spuds & generally tinned fruit. Dinner: - soup, hot meat & two veg, beans & spuds, tinned fruit or sometimes bread pudding, welsh rarebit or sardines, & sometimes coffee. Of course at times we go short of things naturally, but that is not so bad is it? Our quarters are not luxurious & at times tumble down. The poor old feet in the trenches are a lot worse off, though of course they get into rest much oftener. So I hope you won't worry or let the mater worry about my personal comfort.

➜ Henry's drawing of the dugout.

Part of Henry's job was to man field observation posts, elevated positions from which he would direct the fire of the field guns by field telephones. This was an extremely dangerous job, as the officer would be in an exposed position. On 18 September 1918, during an attack on the Germans' Hindenburg Line, Henry was directing fire when the Germans started to shoot at his position.

➔ An officer manning a field observation post during the First World War.

➔ Edward's diary for 1918, showing the entry about Henry's medal.

Henry, in spite of great danger to himself, stayed where he was, directing his battery's fire with great coolness. As a result of this action, his Major recommended him for a medal for bravery. Henry made no mention of this in his letters home until 20 October:

> That owl Evelyn [a fellow officer, not Henry's brother] says he told you about my being put in for a prize, & as nothing more has been heard of it, you have my leave to forget it as it is now undoubtedly a wash out, which is really just as well. I told the Major at the time that it was not worth it. However, I hope you enjoyed a good old gush over it for 5 minutes anyhow.

However, in December, the award of the Military Cross to Henry was published in Army Orders.

Edward was extremely proud of his son's achievement. The words he wrote about it were the most detailed entry that Edward ever made in his diary. The sad thing was that he found it difficult to praise Henry to his face, and Henry never realised how his father felt.

41

AFTER THE WAR

The war had been far longer and far more damaging than anyone had expected in 1914. It was with great relief that people welcomed Germany's surrender on Armistice Day, 11 November 1918.

11 November is still celebrated as a day of remembrance for people who have died fighting in wars since 1914. This photo shows a modern Remembrance Day ceremony in 1995. The wreaths are made of poppies, whose blood-red flowers bloomed in the First World War battlefields of Belgium and France.

Henry stayed in the army until March 1919, and in February of that year he was promoted to Captain. When he was demobilised, Henry returned to the Bank of England. As he was promised when he joined up in August 1914, his job had been kept for him. He found the job boring after his time in the army. He missed the comradeship he had enjoyed with his men and fellow officers when they had been under fire together.

In 1923 Henry married Dorothy Doyle, who had gone to work in the Bank of England during the war, and they had a son and two daughters. In 1928 Dorothy had this letter from her father-in-law Edward:

> 18.9.28
>
> Dear Dorothy,
>
> I am writing to you on Henry's 10th M.C. (Military Cross) day, because I can't praise him to his face, and I can praise him to you; for we must never forget that he was one of the very first in England to enlist in the R.H.A. when he quietly walked out of the Bank on that evening in August 14 years ago; and then after going through the whole War, from Gunner to Captain, he was one of the very last to win his M.C., — "remaining at his observation post under fire, & successfully directing his Battery to break up attack, while in a very exposed position, with great coolness he directed his Brigade fire". That was just 10 years ago today, and then 5 years ago tomorrow you and he were married. It is something to remember isn't it?

KANTARA
SENUSSI
SOMME
MESSINES
NIEUPORT DUNES
PASSCHENDAELE
HOUTHOULST FOREST
ST JULIEN
ANNEQUIN
ARRAS
MAISSEMY
HINDENBURG LINE
SAMBRE CANAL
RHINE
H.M. FROM D.B.
OLLHEIM. 1919.
46TH BATTERY R.F.A.

↑ This is a silver cigarette case which was given to Henry by a fellow officer. All the battles they had been in together are engraved in it. It records not only the history of the war but also their friendship throughout the battles they fought together.

a family story

Some time after the war, a young woman asked Henry what the places engraved in his cigarette case were, and he joked that they were rest stops he had been at during the war. She took him seriously and commented, "Huh! You didn't do much fighting, did you?"

These are the medals awarded to Henry. On the left is his Military Cross, awarded for bravery. The next three, known as 'Pip, Squeak and Wilfred' (after comic strip characters in the *Daily Mirror*), were given to every soldier who was in a particular place at a particular time. 'Pip' or the Mons Star was given to everyone in the war in 1914. 'Squeak' was the General Campaign Medal for those who were in the war between 1914 and 1918, and 'Wilfred' was the Victory Medal given to all soldiers at the end of the war.

⬇ This cemetery is in Belgium, and contains the graves of thousands of British soldiers who fought in the First World War.

➡ This photograph shows Jack's grave in Rossignol Wood cemetery.

Some of the family managed to visit Jack's grave in Belgium, but Evelyn was buried too far away in Iraq for anyone to go.

In April 1919 Edward retired from being vicar at Sutton, and, after a great send-off from the village they had lived in for so many years, he and Lucy moved to Stratford-upon-Avon. On 2 June 1932 Edward recorded Lucy's death in his diary, adding 'beloved by all who knew her'. He died the next year, aged ninety-one.

Henrietta went with her parents to Stratford-upon-Avon. There she met a schoolmaster called Willoughby Smallwood. She married him in 1922, and had two children. Henrietta continued to write to all her brothers until she died in 1980, aged ninety-one. By this time they had written to one another for over eighty years. The Marshall family had been scattered round the world, but, partly thanks to Henrietta, they never let the closeness that they had had as children disappear.

WHAT HAPPENED TO HENRIETTA'S SISTER AND BROTHERS?

Charlie became the Inspector of Mines in Malaya, and died in 1960. Russell continued his work as a medical missionary, but eventually returned to England where he worked as a family doctor. He lived to celebrate his hundredth birthday, but died the following year (1986). Hannath was a missionary in the Bahamas and then a vicar in England. He died in 1964. Frances married a vicar, lived in Norfolk for most of her life, and died in 1960. Arthur returned to England from Malaya and lived in Stratford-upon-Avon, where he was involved in organising Shakespeare festivals. He died in 1936.

Henry remained with the Bank of England, but sadly Dorothy died suddenly in 1942, and, as soon as the Second World War was over in 1945, Henry retired early in order to be at home for his three children. He remained very active all his life, playing hockey for his county until he was in his fifties, and golf well into his eighties. But his four years in the army remained the most important and vivid of his life. In February 1981 he fell and broke his hip. He had to go into hospital for the first time in his life and died a few days later, just before his ninety-third birthday.

Here he is on his eightieth birthday in 1968, surrounded by his son, two daughters, two sons-in-law, his daughter-in-law and nine grandchildren. The author of this book is his daughter-in-law: she is standing at the back, just behind Henry.

It may be possible to spot some family likenesses between this picture and the one taken of the family group in 1897, on page 20.

Glossary

active service to 'see active service' is to take part in fighting during a war

airship a flying machine which uses a balloon filled with gas to keep it in the air

ally/allies country or countries on the same side in a war

armistice the ending of fighting in a war

Armistice Day 11 November 1918, the day on which the agreement to stop fighting in the First World War was signed; the anniversary of that day

Army Orders instructions and information given out by the army every day

artillery very large guns, often moved on wheels

Ascension Day a Christian feast which celebrates the day on which Jesus ascended into heaven

Austria-Hungary in the nineteenth century, Austria and Hungary were one country. Austria-Hungary also had an empire in eastern Europe

batman a soldier who acts as an officer's servant

battalion (Battn) a body of soldiers made up of several **companies**

billets a place where soldiers stay when not fighting

blockade cutting off a place to stop people and supplies going in or out

boarding school a school where the pupils live during term time

brigade a body of troops made up of **regiments** and **battalions**

Brigadier an officer in the army who has charge of a brigade

British Empire countries and **colonies** at one time ruled by Britain

British Expeditionary Force (BEF) the part of the British army (150,000 men) which was the first to be sent to France in 1914

bucked slang for 'really pleased'

bully beef tinned or pickled beef

called up to be 'called up' is to be ordered by the government to join the army

campaign a military operation; an exercise carried out by the army in wartime

Captain (Capt.) an officer who is above a Lieutenant and below a Major

casualties in a war, soldiers who are killed or injured

cavalry soldiers who fight on horseback

censor to check something for information which people in authority believe should be cut out; to cut that information out

chaplain a clergyman (nowadays also a clergywoman) who looks after a group like a regiment or school

Church of England the official Christian organisation in England, its leader being the queen or king

civil servant a person who works for the government

civilian a person who is not in the army, navy or air force

colonial civil service the part of the government that looked after the **colonies**

colonies British colonies were countries at one time ruled by Britain

commanding officer a soldier's commanding officer is the officer who is in overall charge

commission the authority (power) given to an officer to take charge of other soldiers in the army

commissioned officer a soldier who has been given his authority over other soldiers at once, rather than being promoted to officer rank. Commissioned officers are senior to **non-commissioned officers**

company (Coy) part of a regiment

comradeship in this book, 'comradeship' is used to mean close friendship with fellow soldiers, arising from going through terrible experiences together

condolences expressions of sympathy with someone else's sorrow

conscript someone who is forced by the government to serve in the armed forces

conscription getting recruits for the army by legally forcing them to join

convoy a group of warships protecting merchant ships

Corporal a non-commissioned officer below the rank of Sergeant

corroborate to confirm that the information in something is correct by checking it against another source of information

Coy part of a regiment, short for company

croquet a game played on grass which involves using mallets to knock balls through a series of hoops

declaration of war an announcement by a government that it is going to war

demobilised released from the army at the end of a war

drains large canal-like channels in the fens which drain water from the land to the sea

dugout a shelter dug into the side of a trench, perhaps containing a couple of beds and a table, and only for the use of officers

enlist to join the army, navy or air force

entrenched an army which is entrenched has dug and occupied trenches

evacuation withdrawing or removing the army from its previous position, usually because of danger

fag a schoolboy who is forced to do jobs for an older boy

fagging doing the jobs asked for by an older school boy

fen a low, marshy piece of land

field gun a large gun like a modern version of a cannon

field telephone a telephone which could be used on a battlefield. It had a wire which could be wound in and out

firing line the front line of trenches from which the soldiers fired on the enemy

First World War a war which took place between 1914 and 1918 and was fought mostly in Europe and the Middle East

front the area where the two armies in a war are fighting each other

gunner a soldier who works with guns

Hindenburg Line a defensive line of trenches and fortifications made by the Germans towards the end of the First World War

home front a phrase which describes the efforts of people at home to help soldiers fighting abroad win a war

home leave time spent at home by a soldier

infantry soldiers who fight on foot

killed in action killed while fighting in a battle

larder a large cupboard or small room to store food in

Lieutenant / Second Lieutenant officers below the rank of Captain

Lieutenant Colonel officer below the rank of Colonel

light infantry originally, soldiers whose equipment was light enough to allow them to run while carrying it

log book a book, like a diary, in which the records of an organisation like a club or school are kept

Major officer between the rank of Captain and Lieutenant Colonel

mater Latin word for 'mother'

maypole a tall pole with ribbons attached, round which people dance to celebrate the first day of May and the beginning of summer

mess place where officers are served their food

middle class the portion of society which has plenty of money to live on, but isn't extremely rich

Middle East an area which includes most of the countries at the eastern end of the Mediterranean Sea and the countries in the Arabian peninsula

midwife nurse who assists when a baby is born

Military Cross an award for bravery for army officers below the rank of Major

mine a bomb which is left buried in the ground and will explode when trodden on

missionary someone who tries to persuade other people to believe in the missionary's religion

mustard gas a poisonous gas used in the First World War to kill the enemy

nanny a person, in Victorian times always a woman, who looked after someone else's children for them

naval to do with the navy

neutral a neutral country is one which has declared that it will not take part in a particular war

next of kin a person's closest relatives

no man's land neutral land between two fighting forces

non-commissioned officer (NCO) an ordinary soldier who has been promoted from the rank of Private to be in charge of fellow soldiers, usually holding the rank of Corporal or Sergeant

parapet a low wall along the edge of a **trench**

parish a district with its own church

parishioners people who belong to a **parish**

patrol a small group of soldiers going round an area, often at night, looking for dangers and checking enemy positions

'poor old feet' ordinary foot soldiers

preparatory school private school that prepares pupils for their **public school**

Private a soldier who is not an officer or a **non-commissioned officer**

public school a school, often a boarding school, which is not part of the state system of education

rear party soldiers fighting at the back of the army to defend it

reconnaissance the act of getting information about the enemy by sending out aircraft or small groups of soldiers to spy on the enemy

regiment a group of soldiers commanded by a Colonel

Remembrance Day another name for the anniversary of the original **Armistice Day**. On Remembrance Day ceremonies are held to remember the people who have died in wars since 1914.

rubber planter a person who manages an estate where rubber trees are grown

Serbia a country in eastern Europe which **Austria-Hungary** wanted to add to its empire

shells bombs shot from a **field gun**

shrapnel small pieces of metal that injure or kill people when a bomb or shell explodes

sniper a soldier whose job it is to target and shoot individual enemy soldiers

social class some people believe that society is divided into classes of people depending on how wealthy they are and the kinds of jobs they do

surrender to give up, to admit defeat

telegram the written version of a message which has been sent by telegraph – a system of sending messages by radio or electrical signals

tophole slang for 'excellent'

trenches protective ditches dug for the **infantry** in the **First World War**

vicar the priest of a **parish**

volunteer a person who offers to do something without being forced, especially volunteering to join the armed forces (the opposite of a **conscript**)

wired for to wire for someone meant to send them a **telegram** asking them to come to a certain place

Zeppelin a cigar-shaped **airship**

Zepps slang for **Zeppelin**